ROMANCE AND CHIVALRY
IN MODERN SOCIETY

by

G. Lamar Wilkie

This book is dedicated to my Darling Bride Donna, my inspiration to be the most romantic man in the world. For so long as I live, she will go to sleep each night with no doubt about her being the most important person in my life; the most adored and cherished woman on Earth; and the wife of the most blessed and fortunate man alive.

INTRODUCTION

"Of all forms of caution, caution in love is perhaps the most fatal to true happiness." – Bertrand Russell

Despite the mixed messages we may receive, there are timeless, universal truths that never change. One is that most women desire a relationship with a man who is confident; faithful; protective of her but not controlling; and who will treat her like royalty. She will be his loyal and faithful companion for life.

Sadly, most men aren't taught <u>how</u> to be that "knight in shining armor" for their lady. Our modern culture has almost completely erased the words *"romance"* and *"chivalry"* from the vocabulary, although both are crucial for relating with others... especially with women.

You may never have been taught etiquette and courtesy: perhaps you've been told that you have a romance deficiency. While the truth can hurt, it illuminates opportunity for improvement. Either way, this book can help you find that romantic deep within you–and bring him out to change *your* life for the better, as well as those around you.

Love is not a spectator sport, however–you've got to get in the game!

Here's a disclaimer up front: I am not a certified counselor, nor do I pretend to be. I'm just an old-fashioned romantic who feels this is important for someone to read. I've been the unashamed, romantic husband to my Darling Bride Donna since 1990.

That's not a typo... 1990.

I'll be sharing a few concepts with you, as well as some thoughts and romantic ideas to help make your relationship better, stronger, and more enjoyable.

ROMANCE AND CHIVALRY IN MODERN SOCIETY

Let's get started.

Chapter 1

IMPORTANT THINGS TO KNOW

"I am my beloved's, and my beloved is mine." – Song of Solomon

#1 – Romance is NOT about sex! If you're looking for ideas to score quick, easy sex, this is not the book for you.

Quick, easy sex is like a microwave meal. It may do the job, but only barely. It is neither satisfying nor memorable.

Romance is like a home-cooked meal, with every dish lovingly prepared from scratch and cooked slowly. It's rich, fulfilling and oh, so satisfying.

Why?

Emotion. When two people have quick, easy sex it's only a physical exchange. That's all. However, when two people have been slowly building their relationship; when they understand each other's needs, dreams, and fears; when their desire to be together has been increasing in mutual respect and love, then their physical intimacy becomes so much more powerful.

That's what romance is: it's a long-lasting exchange of loving interactions that forms the basis for the most successful relationships. It takes a long time–often years–to form a deep, romantic relationship, but it's very much worth it.

#2 – Romance is NOT about <u>you</u>, or what <u>you</u> can get out of it. It's about <u>her</u> and what you can do for <u>her</u>. The more effort you pour into showing her that she is the most important person in your life and the center of your world, the more she will come to respond to you in the same way. It requires considerable investment in time and effort. You should always, however, romance your Lady with zero expectation of receiving anything in return.

#3 – Romance is NOT an activity! It's a mindset: your way of life. Romance isn't something you *do*... it's something you *are*. If you have a romantic philosophy, everyone around you will know it without your saying a word. They will see it: and they will want to experience more of it, because romance is simply that important.

Chapter 2

HOW DO I MEET THAT SPECIAL LADY?

"There is only one happiness in life: to love and be loved." – George Sand

Today's culture is running at an insane pace. It's not just the change that's driving people into seclusion: it's the dizzying *rate* of change. We're bombarded with information from the time we wake up until the time we finally fall asleep. We often wake up still exhausted, because our minds didn't have enough time to process everything from yesterday.

Almost everything is available online, and that is a tragic reality. There is nothing social about "social media", either, because we're all detached from each other... and that's not how we're created to operate. We humans are social creatures: we have been since the dawn of time, and we need to be around other people to feel truly human. Yes, even introverts need someone else close to them.

Remember reading, back in the Introduction, that love is not a spectator sport? It's more of a full contact sport. Full contact with another, special person: with eyes locked, smiles, gentle touches and one-on-one communication.

Breaking the cycle of living exclusively online and alone, and shifting to real-world/in-person, can be both exciting and terrifying. The rewards, however, are a closer bond with the person or people you are with. Nothing is better than being right next to that special woman you care about most... and who equally cares for you right back.

How to meet her, though?

First, you need to determine the *type* of woman you might want to meet... and then go to the places where those types of women might likely be found. If you prefer a well-read, knowledgeable woman, frequent your local library or bookshop. If you want someone who focuses on wellness and athletics, try the gym. If you want someone who values faith, find a church you feel comfortable with and join a single adults group there.

Whatever you do, you <u>must</u> follow these primary rules:

BE YOURSELF! As soon as you try to be someone you're not, people will know. It's very difficult to recover from a bad reputation... so just be real. There's a special someone out there for each of us, no matter who we are.

BE SINCERE! If you're trying to flatter a woman by showering her with compliments that aren't true, she's going to see right through it. Sincerity is absolutely essential.

BE APPROACHABLE! That means being meticulous about your grooming and hygiene. Be clean and neat: look good, smell good, wear nice, clean clothes. Don't stare at your phone or another screen: make it obvious that you're someone with whom a woman might enjoy sitting down and talking.

BE POLITE! No one likes a creepy guy who acts like he's desperate to get into a woman's panties, so he starts flirting right away. Don't be that guy! Remember: this isn't about sex... it's about relationship.

And let's talk about that:

What is romance, anyway? If it's not about sex or flirting, then what is it? What's the difference?

Sex is about making love to someone's body.

G. LAMAR WILKIE

Flirting is about making love to someone's mind.

Romance is about making love to someone's <u>heart</u>.

To be successful in an intimate relationship, you need to practice those arts in this order: romance, then flirting, and then—much later—sex.

Chapter 3

CHIVALRY

"To the world you may be just one person, but to one person you may be the world." – Brandi Snyder

You may hear the term "chivalry", which was very common in times past. Chivalry is simply the art of treating every man as a gentleman, and every woman as a Lady. I encourage you to read more about chivalry and practice it as a lifestyle: you will instantly stand out from among your contemporaries; women you don't even know will start to hear about you. They will eventually start seeking you out!

The term "gentleman" might seem old-fashioned in our modern era, but here's a little secret: chivalry works! Modern gentlemen regularly practice the virtues of chivalry, and our efforts are appreciated by the vast majority of women.

Why would you treat every man like a gentleman and every woman like a Lady, however... especially if they don't act like a gentleman or Lady?

There is a little-known, and often overlooked, principle known as "Psychological Reciprocity" and it applies to almost everyone you will ever meet in life. Psychological Reciprocity is simply this:

If you give a person credit for who he or she is, then he or she is mentally and morally obligated to give you credit for who you are.

You can easily apply this principle in almost any situation, with anyone, if you understand basic human emotional needs:

- Everyone needs affirmation as an individual
- Everyone needs to love and be loved
- Everyone needs to feel important, to someone, in some way

Consider a social situation in which you are conducting yourself like a gentleman while another man around you conducts himself poorly: telling crude jokes, using profanity, insulting or disrespecting others. In contrast, you conduct yourself in proper manner: asking open questions and courteously treating others as more important than yourself. You use clean language and politely engage others in meaningful conversation.

If you treat him like a gentleman and acknowledge that his potential is so much greater than he is currently demonstrating, he will almost always rise to your level of conduct, since he cannot successfully bring you down to his. He quickly realizes that he will seem awful in comparison to you. He genuinely wants to be recognized for who he can be, not necessarily who he is in the here and now, though he may not understand how to improve. By employing Psychological Reciprocity, he will eventually begin to treat you like a gentleman as well, and start cleaning up his conduct, even if he doesn't immediately realize he's doing it.

We are products of our environment... and popular culture is most horrible teacher of courtesy. He may be so influenced by our culture's "race to the bottom" that he simply needs confirmation that he *can* improve; that there *is* a higher standard to which he can successfully aspire.

Consider even small courtesies–hold the door for her, give her your seat, pay for her dinner, refresh her drink, or help her carry things.

As hard as we try, though, we're human and we all make mistakes. When they do, it's crucial that you immediately "fess up when you mess up", apologize, and try to explain your sincere intentions. People may misread your honest mistake as a sexually suggestive act.

THIS IS IMPORTANT: the sleazy pick-up artist and the true gentleman are completely OPPOSITE types of men!

It's also important to remember that *genuine* masculinity protects, provides for, and brings out the best of femininity: allowing women to flourish and grow to their highest female potential. There are critical attributes in proper manliness that are comforting to women. They feel protected. They feel loved and cared for. They feel empowered to be their best as a woman.

So, what makes a person chivalrous?

Chivalry is an evolved form of medieval knighthood: defending the innocent and protecting Ladies at all costs. In the post-medieval days, chivalry formed the basis of gentlemanly conduct. While classical chivalry doesn't really apply in our modern era, many of its ideals still feel right. This *chivalric code* guides the way the modern gentleman treats others, because that's how we conduct our lives. This is especially true of your Lady: she deserves nothing less.

French historian Léon Gautier compiled the first "Ten Commandments of Chivalry" in 1891. They're generally self-explanatory and common-sense. Be firm in your convictions; defend those who cannot defend themselves; be courageous and patriotic; stand resolute against opposition; volunteer and be involved in local civics; be honest and never break a promise; give of yourself to causes about which you are passionate; and be a force for morality and uprightness.

While George Washington is said to have written "*Rules of Civility & Decent Behavior In Company and Conversation*" in his teen years, he only did so as a handwriting exercise as part of his education. It was copied, word for word, from a 1640 book of the same title by Francis

Hawkins, who had translated a 1595 book by French Jesuits, similarly titles "*Bienséance de la Conversation Entre les Hommes*".

It's a very short book with only 110 Rules, most of which are a single sentence. It would do you great credit to read it and apply those Rules to your own life, as the first President of the United States lived by those Rules as his personal code of conduct.

Here are a few ways anyone can demonstrate modern chivalry:

1. BE COURTEOUS. Former Senator and U.S. Vice President Albert Gore, Jr. once commissioned a study, titled "World Class Courtesy", on the positive effects of courtesy in the workplace. Why would he do that?

Because common, thoughtful courtesy works. It's a best practice! I'm sure you would prefer that someone doesn't shut a door in your face or cut you off while driving in traffic. Don't do those things yourself! If someone treats you rudely, respond to them with civility. The Bible refers to this as "heaping fiery coals on their head" because of the sense of conviction those rude people will eventually feel when you repay their rudeness with kindness. It's a response they didn't expect, and it perplexes them, in a good way! They may completely rethink their social behavior.

2. BE HONEST. Chivalry is a pathway to deeper and more satisfying personal interactions; honesty is the cornerstone of any relationship you build.

You can't build relationships with other people without personal integrity. Be truthful with yourself and others. Look beyond your own words, however, and consider how it feels for the other person to hear them. Sometimes the truth hurts: be honest, yes: but be diplomatic in the way you communicate a painful truth.

3. BE HELPFUL. Everyone needs help occasionally and chivalry means helping people without patronizing them:

"Can I help you find something?"

"That looks heavy/bulky. Please, let me carry that for you."

One example is if someone is in the checkout line ahead of you in the grocery store. She has small children with her. Her items are evidence that the children are hers and she's trying her best to provide for them. If she cannot pay for the groceries and, embarrassed, asks the cashier to begin removing items until she can afford them, that's your cue to step in. If you have the means, tell the cashier that you will pay for her groceries. All of them. If you can't pay for everything, pay what she can't. When the struggling mother looks at you with astonishment, let her know that you appreciate the sacrifices she's making for her kids, and it's your privilege to help her. *That's* chivalry.

Another example is if an elderly or disabled person is trying to reach something on an upper shelf. Ask what they're trying to get, reach up and get it for them. Ask if there's anything else you can help with.

It's very possible that you were meant to be in that place, at that moment, for that reason.

Ask and pay attention to the ways other people like for you to step in and assist (and ways they don't). This is particularly true about your partner or prospective life mate. As you learn about their needs (and, likewise, communicate your own to them), you grow more sensitive to each other.

4. BE COMPASSIONATE. How do you respond to things like homelessness, abuse, or addiction? Whether you keep energy bars in your car to give a homeless person while offering to help access social

resources; or volunteer to help the local animal shelter or a veterans' organization, others need to know that you have compassion for others.

In practicing chivalry, as in every other aspect of life, perception is 95% of a person's reality. It's crucial for your success in life that others have a positive perception of you. Here are two of the most effective things you can do to improve others' perception of you:

#1 – Make it a point to learn something new, about something, every single day of your life.

It can be on any topic: but just don't settle into one topic. Learn something about geography one day; astronomy the next; chemistry the next; and so on. Eventually, you will gain a basic understanding of almost every subject. If there's an aspect you don't quite understand, research that aspect until you do (it's neither difficult nor time-consuming). You will be able to hold your own in virtually any conversation you have, with anyone, about anything. This will serve to enhance your general reputation as a knowledgeable and educated person who treats everyone respectfully and equally.

In doing this, if you encounter a word or term that you don't understand, STOP and look it up. Learn what it means, and how to use it properly. This will not only make your understanding of the subject matter clearer in the moment: but increasing your vocabulary will make future learning easier. Increasing your vocabulary will also make it easier for you to both comprehend others in conversation and express your own views... even if it's a complex topic.

At the same time, if someone begins talking about a subject with which you are not familiar, it's perfectly okay to ask them for more information! Rare is the person who would be unwilling to share his or her knowledge: asking someone to teach you more about a subject is flattering to them and beneficial to you. It's a win-win conversation!

Of course, when you have the option of using either a bigger word or a smaller word, use the *smaller* word every time. There's no need to prove your extensive vocabulary to other people! For example, you shouldn't say the word "utilize" if the word "use" is perfectly okay in the sentence. How many times have we heard someone use complicated words or terms, knowing they do it just to prove they can? It can come across as annoying and arrogant... so don't be that person.

#2 – Find a cause about which you are passionate and a local charity for that cause, and volunteer.

Service to others through volunteer work is a hallmark of good citizenship. It takes our focus away from self and opens doors of opportunity that we never knew existed.

Not only will you come to feel much better about yourself by helping the less fortunate, or promoting a cause you hold dearly, but others will see your passion and share your energy & enthusiasm. It's very possible that you'll meet that special someone through your volunteer efforts. You have a common passion: but varied interests. Volunteering often rewards us with so much more than we give in time, money and effort... in this case, it may reward you for a lifetime! Stay open to other opportunities that may come your way: from employment to leadership positions, you never know who will notice your efforts, so make them noble.

As a young man, Benjamin Franklin made a list of 13 virtues. He committed himself to achieving moral perfection: but discovered that doing so was impossible because, in his words, "habit took advantage of inattention." He then strived to break bad habits, and establish good ones in their place, by refining one virtue at a time for an entire year. After 13 years, Franklin was at the peak of his productivity, scientific ingenuity, wit, and charm. This served him well for the rest of his life: as an emissary to England before the Revolution for American Independence and to France during the conflict, he was a much sought-after man... not only for his knowledge and keen understanding, but also his enjoyable company. Practice these virtues as listed by Franklin: you will be indispensable to many, and highly desirable to some:

Temperance: Eat not to dullness. Drink not to elevation.

Silence: Speak not but what may benefit others or yourself. Avoid trifling conversation.

Order: Let all your things have their places. Let each part of your business have its time.

Resolution: Resolve to perform what you ought. Perform without fail what you resolve.

Frugality: Make no expense but to do good to others or yourself: waste nothing.

Industry: Lose no time. Be always employed in something useful. Cut off all unnecessary actions.

Sincerity: Use no hurtful deceit. Think innocently and justly; and, if you speak, speak accordingly.

Justice: Wrong none, by doing injuries or omitting the benefits that are your duty.

Moderation: Avoid extremes. Forbear resenting injuries so much as you think they deserve.

Cleanliness: Tolerate no uncleanliness in body, clothes, or home.

Tranquility: Be not disturbed at trifles, or at accidents common or unavoidable.

Chastity: Rarely exercise sexual gratification but for health or offspring; never to dullness, weakness, or the injury of your own or another's peace or reputation.

Humility: Imitate Jesus and Socrates.

ROMANCE AND CHIVALRY IN MODERN SOCIETY

(While reading that list of virtues, did you encounter a word or term you didn't understand? Did you look it up to learn its meaning?)

Chapter 4

BODY LANGUAGE

"I would rather have eyes that cannot see; ears that cannot hear; lips that cannot speak, than a heart that cannot love." – Robert Tizon

One critical aspect of romance and chivalry is reading the nonverbal cues you receive from other people. Having a better understanding of body language will not only help you perceive other people more effectively: you will also be more aware of how you are being perceived by them.

There are two primary principles of body language, the first being the 55/38/7 Rule. While it's not necessary to remember those specific numbers, it is necessary to understand how each number relates to the others.

Our words, the things we actually SAY to someone, only account for 7% of our total communication with them. HOW we say those words accounts for 38% of our total communication (vocal pitch, inflection, and speed). The remaining 55% of our communication is nonverbal: appearance, posture, gestures, and facial expressions.

That's right: the majority of human communication involves no talking at all... that's how important body language is!

It may serve you well to take a course, or watch video lessons, on public speaking: for no other reason than to become more proficient at the verbal part of your communication. By being more articulate in your speech, you can better control 45% of the conversation.

The nonverbal 55% of the conversation is more difficult to control because much of it is subliminal. We will often send cues to the other person without even knowing we're doing it.

This chapter is crucial, then, in helping you to better understand nonverbal communication. Not only will it help you understand others, but you can become more aware of the signals your body is sending out to them.

In understanding the relationship between the 55%, the 38% and the 7% of conversation, the second principle, known as "The 3 C's", can be of great value.

These are Context, Cluster, and Congruence.

Context is important because a person sending nonverbal cues to your communication may not be reacting you what you're saying at all. If someone yawns during your conversation, it doesn't necessarily mean that person finds you boring. He or she may actually be very tired. Someone crossing their arms may simply be cold, and not doing so as a negative posture.

Cluster is the consideration of all three aspects of their communication, and not just one. You must consider their words <u>and</u> behaviors together and make a more accurate determination than you can from one aspect or another.

Congruence simply means that we humans subconsciously place the highest priority on the largest part of the conversation: nonverbal. Words are important... but someone's words, speech and body language should all match (in other words, they should be *congruent*).

If there's a perceived contradiction between what someone says and how they're saying it, the larger number wins.

Consider finding a man seated in the park. He is slumped over and trembling, his face is pale, and he seems to be struggling to breathe. When you ask him if he's okay or needs help, he quietly responds that he's perfectly fine and doesn't need assistance.

Would you take him at his word and walk away? Or does his nonverbal communication tell you he may be in medical distress? If you're like most, you would stay with him while calling for help. This is the principle of Congruence in action: he gave you conflicting information and his nonverbal communication was more important than his words.

Be very aware of these two principles: pay attention to HOW people say things, rather than merely WHAT they're saying, and you will gain control of the conversation by knowing how to steer it. You'll no longer react to what's being said: you will be able to perceive how the other person is reacting. You will also be more aware of how you are being perceived.

Try this for practice: go to a coffee shop, restaurant, or other public place where various conversations are going on. You needn't say anything: just observe and read the body language people send to each other. Practice being aware of what people communicate nonverbally. As you observe, you'll notice that body language will be either open or closed.

Open body language may involve one's hands in view, with palms up and open. This is a subliminal cue of vulnerability—there's a level of comfort and trust in the conversation. Direct eye contact is open body language: the person is receptive to the speaker, what's being said, and how it's communicated. Our eyes are windows to our soul. When two people lock eyes, they are gazing into one another on a deep and intimate level.

Closed body language is defensive. We put up a wall, either physical or psychological, against something we perceive is a threat... even if there is no direct threat. Remember that perception is 95% of reality to a person. If he or she feels badly about a conversation, their arms/legs will be close to the body or even crossed. They will avoid eye contact, looking away or even closing their eyes, indicating that they are not receptive.

Have you ever walked quickly past a salesperson while avoiding eye contact?

Eye contact is *extremely* powerful: too much of it, however, can have a negative effect. If someone stares into your eyes but never releases their gaze, you may begin thinking they're trying too hard and are desperate for something. There's a balance, then, between no eye contact and too much of it.

Make eye contact, absolutely: but avert your gaze, ever so slightly, to occasionally break that soul-to-soul connection. This allows the other person to subconsciously "rest". This is extremely important! By breaking your gaze from time to time, it gives them permission to break theirs. The conversation will be more natural and enjoyable for everyone.

As a romantic, you will want to avert your gaze and either look at her hair or ears, a nearby object, or perhaps settle it on her lips or just below her chin, where her necklace might be... just for a moment, and then look back into her eyes. The one thing you don't want to look at is her chest. Chivalry means treating a woman like a human being, and not an object of desire.

A tremendous amount of research has been conducted simply on eye contact: you would benefit greatly from learning a little more about it than this book will cover.

So far, we have discussed the person sending the communication, but it takes two: the sender and the receiver. Actively listening has its own body language. You will know if your listener is focused on what you have to say... if you're aware of what to look for. There's no point in continuing a conversation without an engaged audience!

Being an active listener includes nodding to show encouragement, or that you're still listening and paying attention. A nod may also indicate that you understand, it may say "yes" to a question or that you agree with a statement.

A lack of nodding can cause the speaker to think you're not paying attention, or you're not interested. In fact, some studies have shown that actively nodding can extract up to four times more information than the speaker had intended to give!

Next, try to mimic someone's body language... without completely copying them move for move. That way, you can lead them into a more open posture. Be aware of your own closed posture, especially if you disagree with something, as it can lead them to copy you!

One of the most effective ways to lead a conversation positively is to use a lot of hand gestures. Having your palms up, as opposed to down or at your side, is body language that tells them "I trust you and can be honest with you." Listeners will interpret your communication more positively.

People tend to associate an open palm with friendliness, honesty, and trust. On the opposite side, palms down or a pointed finger conveys dominance or authority. Clasped arms convey a state of conflict and tension. The higher the hands are, the higher the resistance.

People are conditioned to turn towards things and people we like. If a woman is flirting with more than one guy, check which one her lower body is facing and you'll know immediately who interests her more.

Conversely, if you're in a conversation and the person turns their lower body, it could be that they want or need to leave. Don't underestimate the lower body! People can force a smile or control some nonverbal communication: but people are less trained further down the body.

Finally, proximity is very important. You can often tell how close two people are based on how close they are physically.

We all have our own personal zone around us, however; and you may be immediately rejected if you enter someone's personal zone too quickly and without permission. Keep a respectful distance.

Chapter 5

FINDING HER

""Love and compassion are necessities, not luxuries. Without them, humanity cannot survive." – the 14th Dalai Lama

You may encounter many "hers" in your search for The One destined to be your life mate. Rule number one is to <u>not</u> look at those women with whom you share many things in common. Don't exclude anyone but start your short list with the women with whom you may feel opposed on just about everything!

EXAMPLE: after a three-year tour aboard a United States Navy warship, including an incredible six-month deployment to the South Pacific, I was transferred to Naples, Italy where I was assigned to a barracks where a certain woman, also in the Navy, worked. I will quickly tell you (she will, too) that we immediately despised each other with a fury.

It was our mission to make each other miserable. We were polar opposites: I was the free-spirited daredevil, and she was the "rules and regulations" type of person. For her, everything had to be "by the book". I'm not sure I ever <u>read</u> "the book".

After about a year of this hostility, we essentially dared ourselves to make a 3-day road trip together over to the east coast of Italy. It was on that trip that we learned we had a lot more in common than we had ever thought possible. Over a relatively short period of time, spite turned to understanding, to acceptance, to like, and finally, to love.

I was successful in helping her "loosen up" and enjoy life more; and she was successful in grounding me more in reality. We shared a wonderful synergy.

We ran together for the next two years: exploring the Italian backroads, meeting great people, and enjoying fantastic food, wine, and scenery. Two years after that I proposed to her. We married in 1990 and we're more madly in love now than ever. We're also still "sparring partners" and trade loving barbs to keep things lively (without being hurtful).

Just remember: if two people in a relationship are exactly the same, one is unnecessary... right?

Here's another rule: physical attraction is no basis for a relationship. That doesn't mean you should attach yourself to someone you find repulsive... it means that beauty is fleeting and doesn't last. A lasting relationship is built on personality and the chemistry the two of you share together.

Make sure, very early in your observation of a woman you would like to approach, that she is not wearing an engagement or wedding ring. If she is, you're too late! Some other lucky guy won her heart first... so keep looking! Don't try to get cozy with someone else's fiancé or spouse, because you wouldn't want someone trying to get cozy with yours!

It may take some practice to become comfortable with approaching women in our age. It's okay: many will be pleasantly surprised by your attention! A woman often spends a lot of time, money, and effort to look nice: it's okay to recognize her efforts. Complimenting a woman is not a bad thing!

When a woman makes eye contact with you, hold your gaze for a moment. Smile and look away at something–then look back. If the two of you lock eyes again, smile. Nothing crazy... just a sincere smile.

ROMANCE AND CHIVALRY IN MODERN SOCIETY

Look at her. What is it about her that's notable? Say "hi" to her and offer a sincere compliment. It may be about her choice of hairstyle; it may be an interesting outfit or piece of jewelry she chose to wear. Something to start the conversation! Let her know what you find interesting and let her tell you about it.

Introduce yourself and smile. Admit that you're not used to walking up to women you've never met and starting a conversation: but there's something in her eyes that just compelled you to say hello.

She may be flattered. Hopefully she'll respond with her name and admit she's not used to it, either. Ask open questions like, "what do you do for a living? Where are you from originally? Wow, that's so interesting!" If you noticed her outfit or jewelry, tell her it's very interesting to you; and ask her what compelled her to wear that today. If she asks, tell her a little about yourself.

She may be intimidated and shy away, thinking you're trying to sell her something or otherwise take advantage of her. This could very well happen, especially if she's just gotten out of an abusive situation and isn't ready for such attention. If she doesn't respond positively, apologize as she darts away and consider it practice. It's okay–she's just not The One!

If she *does* respond positively, you might feel emboldened enough to apologize for taking so much of her time: but you feel so comfortable talking with her that you'd love to continue the conversation. Offer your cell number: ask for hers, and promise you'll text her within minutes, so she has your number.

She may not give you her number but would like yours. It's up to you, then, to decide whether to give it to her. She may not be interested in exchanging numbers... and that's okay! You complimented a total stranger, she appreciated it, and that's great! Thank her for her time and let her know that you hope to meet her again someday soon. Again, consider it practice and another opportunity to gain confidence.

If she gives you her number, make sure you text her <u>immediately</u> after you part ways! Don't wait until you get home or even leave the establishment... send it right then and there. The message may be as simple as:

"Hi (her name), this is (your name). As promised, here is my number. It was great meeting you! I was so nervous walking up to you like that and saying something, but I'm glad I did. I look forward to hearing from you."

If she responds and says she felt equally comfortable with you, you might ask her when would be a good time for a quick phone call. If she replies and you later call her, tell her it's great to talk with her and hear her voice again: ask where her favorite coffee shop is; and that perhaps you can meet there and chat a little more when she has some free time.

This is NOT a date: it's an <u>audition</u> for a date! It's a safe, public place to meet where the two of you can talk more and decide if the other is dateable. If you get along well there, have lots to talk about and share a few common interests (or even different interests that inspire further conversation), then perhaps you can agree on a follow-up.

The most important thing you need to be aware of (and, sadly, most people aren't) is the chemistry you share with her. If you look deeply into her eyes and see the layers of her soul; if you touch her hand and feel electric fire jump between you, that's something you need to value more than anything else. If you feel it, chances are she feels it. And that's magical.

Smile. A LOT. Nothing creepy: but eye contact and sincere smiles are crucial nonverbal conversation. Money and a flashy lifestyle may buy some quick flesh for the players... but they will never buy a woman's <u>heart</u>. Romance does. Chivalry does.

ROMANCE AND CHIVALRY IN MODERN SOCIETY

Humor is a trait that women value highly in a man. If you can inject some humor into the conversation (especially a little self-deprecating humor), it can go a long way to winning her heart. People need to laugh; and they need know that the person they're with doesn't take themselves too seriously. Life is short: have fun!

Women also value intelligence! That can be greatly improved by referring back to chivalry and the most effective thing you can do to improve others' perception of you: learn something new, about something, every day. If you can make her laugh and engage her in meaningful conversation about any subject, you already hold two of the three keys to her heart. The third is *romance.*

Frequently address her by name. Not only will this help cement her name into your memory, but Robert C. Lee said that the sweetest sound a person can hear is the sound of their own name. Let her hear you say her name to her.

Talk about her, not you! Pay close attention to her interests–this is where chivalry becomes important. If she likes a certain music group or genre, then finding an event with that music, to which you can invite her, will impress her in that you *listened* to what she was saying. That's a huge plus in this day of artificial people having superficial conversations. It's easy to *hear* people talking, but it takes effort to concentrate and *listen* to what someone is saying to us! If she knows you are listening and paying attention to what she's saying to you, she will respect you and your sincerity that much more.

Chapter 6

I KNOW THIS WOMAN, BUT HOW DO I...?

"Love is our true destiny. We do not find the meaning of life by ourselves alone—we find it with another." – Thomas Merton

What if you already know a woman? Either at work or school... perhaps in your civic or church group?

The rules are the same, but with some additional boundaries.

If you both work for the same company, the most important thing is to ensure that you both are on the same level of responsibility. Most companies have policies against fraternization: that is, a relationship between personnel, especially those in supervisory/subordinate positions, that is unduly familiar. It may not matter that you're in completely different departments. You don't want to get fired by romancing her; and you definitely don't want HER getting fired. That is contrary to chivalry.

This is a case in which you will certainly want to consult your company's human resources office for guidance. If you feel attracted to her and truly believe you may be her ONE, and she is yours, but you're in a senior/subordinate situation that prohibits a romantic relationship, then immerse yourself in learning more, taking on additional duties, etc. until you are promoted to the same leadership level that she's in. Then, and only then, can you even begin to court her.

If you are already on an equivalent level of responsibility or leadership, these rules apply:

First, just be friendly and courteous. Always ask open questions (not those with simple "yes" or "no" answers): does she have a significant other? She may not be interested or has recently gotten out of a relationship and isn't ready for another one. Don't move in too quickly!

Ease in with conversation and get a good feel for what she's going through in her life. Respect her boundaries and ask questions about those aspects of her life she feels comfortable discussing.

If she's had horrible experiences with men (tragically, too many wonderful women have), then empathize with her. Don't sympathize or try to apologize on behalf of all men but let her know you understand. So many young women get pregnant, and the fathers run from their responsibilities. After several generations of this social tragedy, there are few (if any) standards of conduct remaining. **If boys don't learn, men won't know!** Let her know that while you feel badly about what happened to her in the past, you are the exact opposite of that behavior and hope to gain her trust.

Second, it's perfectly okay to get to know people better: that's how we make friends. If your conversation and questions stay in that zone, things should feel comfortable for both of you. When she's more at ease with you and you have begun sharing some of the more personal aspects of your life, she may share more of hers. Let her take her time and do this at *her* pace... not yours.

Third, keep the focus on HER! Address her by name and show her that you're sincerely interested in learning more about her. People love to talk about themselves, so let her. Topics you can freely discuss are:

- Occupation—what does she do? What caused her to select that occupation? What sort of long-term career goals does she have, and how is she advancing to achieve them? What obstacles, if any, does she perceive?

- Hobbies—what does she enjoy doing in her free time? Does she write, quilt, or rope cattle? Does she play any musical instruments? Does she love cars or computers, kittens, or dolphins? Does she volunteer or help with any non-profit organizations?

- Family—does her family live nearby? What do they enjoy doing together? What about them drives her crazy? (Be ready to answer that one yourself) Does she have pets? What kind, and what are their names? They may be her current family, so treat them as such. Remember her pet's name because it's important for her. Make it important for you, as well! Ask about them when you see or talk with her.

- Travel—where has she been that she found an incredible experience... and why? Are there any special places she'd love to go?

ROMANCE AND CHIVALRY IN MODERN SOCIETY

Some topics are NOT okay:

Try to not dwell or focus on the negative things in either of your pasts. Don't avoid them but keep your conversations as positive and uplifting as possible.

Don't mention anything sexual or even suggestive–this is a BIG NO! This has nothing to do with sex, so don't go anywhere near the subject! If she starts getting suggestive, don't give in to the temptation. Change the subject: YOU control the conversations that you have! In short: if it's a topic you would feel uncomfortable discussing with a priest, or your grandparents, don't discuss it with her... not at this point!

If you work at the same company with this woman, you will always remain subject to policies against sexual harassment even if you are not subject to policies against fraternization. Sexual harassment is unwanted/unsolicited advances of a sexual nature. This can even be a crime if someone communicates potential professional advantages or disadvantages to another in exchange for intimate favors.

Once again: this is not about sex, so stay as far away from the subject as possible until you are much, much farther along into a relationship!

Chapter 7

THE DATE

"I love you not only for what you are, but for what I am when I am with you." – Elizabeth Barrett Browning

When you finally feel comfortable enough to invite her to share a meal together, or go dancing, or even attend that concert or movie you both want to see, it's important that you make it a special and memorable occasion for her. This is your moment to shine!

Dress the part. That doesn't mean you have to wear a suit or rent a tuxedo (unless the occasion calls for one), but don't show up in old jeans and t-shirt. Shower, shave, get a nice haircut a few days in advance. Make sure you look and smell good: that means a nice, masculine cologne that's barely noticeable and not overpowering.

You may have to invest time experimenting with various fragrances to find a few that work well with your personal body chemistry. Since you are immune to your own personal scent (and we all have one), it's important to have someone in your life, perhaps a coworker or family member, who will truthfully tell you if a cologne works well for you or if it conflicts. Once you have a small repertoire of fragrances that are compatible with you, then you can choose one based on your wardrobe, your mood, and the occasion.

ROMANCE AND CHIVALRY IN MODERN SOCIETY

Wear nice slacks, socks & shoes, and a collared shirt. Make it a priority: put time and effort into being a good date for her to be seen with, because chances are she's putting time and effort into being a good date for you.

Show up EARLY. If you say you will meet her at 6 PM, be there no later than 5:50 PM. The point is to respect her time. Don't ever be late! If you are delayed for an unavoidable reason (traffic or another emergency), call her as early as possible to let her know.

Consider a small gift for her. It could be a small bottle of her favorite wine, or even a favorite chocolate/candy of hers. Even if it's a treat for her pet, just let her know it's a token of your appreciation for the time she has chosen to spend with you.

While on the date, be ever the gentleman. This goes back to chivalry and treating her like royalty. Open the car door for her. Hold doors open and hold her seat while she sits. Pay for her meal, or ticket, or whatever. Unless she *insists* on paying her own way, you pay. NEVER use profanity or even coarse language on a date! Never!

You may be the only man in the place doing all this. It's perfectly fine to be a trendsetter and demonstrate a good example of chivalry. Be the kind of man she would love to marry and spend the rest of her life with... even if you're not him. Your objective in this is to be the kind of date that she will boast about–not complain about–to her friends and coworkers.

Respect her time. If she needs to be at work in the morning, don't keep her out until midnight. Have her home in time for her to get some good sleep. When the date is over, do NOT expect a kiss! Take her hand gently, place your other hand on top of hers; lock eyes with her and smile; sincerely thank her for a most wonderful time; and tell her you hope she enjoyed it as much as you did and that you'd love to do it again soon. Politely bid her good night's sleep and leave.

She may ask, as you turn to leave, why you're not kissing her. Let her know you respect her far too much to assume that from her: but if she would like a kiss, you would consider it a privilege. Such an expression of respect for her flies in the face of popular culture and may pleasantly surprise her. She may simply thank you for an incredible evening and bid you goodnight as well.

If she tells you she would like a kiss, then look into her eyes with a simple smile of gratitude. Move closer, perhaps touch your hand to the side of her face and give her a nice, simple kiss. A "nice, simple kiss" is touching your lips to hers with just enough suction to attract her lips to yours... but just a little bit. No open mouth or tongue—just a nice kiss on the lips! Then back away, look into her eyes and let her know it was far better than you could have ever imagined. You can even whisper something like, "that was incredible..."

If she moves in for another kiss, great! Let her kiss you and meet her in that kiss: this time, gently stroke the sides of her head with your hands, running your fingers through her hair. If she opens her mouth a little, open yours a little. If she darts her tongue toward yours, let the tip of your tongue meet hers. DO NOT try licking her tonsils—this is a romantic kiss, not a tongue-swallowing contest! Keep most of your tongue to yourself and just enjoy the taste of her kiss! Tell her that her kiss is the sweetest thing you've ever tasted. Be ever the gentleman, even in the middle of a passionate kiss.

If things quickly get serious, stop and back off. Save the serious things for later! Just smile and thank her for the most wonderful ending to a most wonderful evening. Trust me in this: take your time: if it makes both of you miserable to wait, it's still far better than doing something either of you may later regret.

Follow up your date with a text or email the next morning, thanking her again for a wonderful time (and if you kissed, for a most intoxicating kiss you can't stop thinking about). Then hope she responds with a similar message. If not, don't keep texting her. You'll see her again and, when you do, just sincerely ask her if she had any regrets about your time together. It's much easier to read her body language in person.

If she communicates something that she found regretful, apologize to her (even if you did nothing wrong) and let her know that her regret was never your intention. Resolve to be mindful of her feelings in the future and tell her that you hope to enjoy her company again sometime soon, and ensure she has nothing but a wonderful time.

If you believe she is The One, you will be patient and wait for her. She may make it very clear to you that she isn't the woman for you... if she does, then respectfully thank her for her honesty and LET HER GO! If there is one thing I learned in the Navy, it's that you can't push a rope–likewise, you can't force a person to be someone they aren't or consider you someone you aren't! There are billions of available women out there, many in your vicinity. Start over and be grateful for your experience with her. If you work with her, then continue treating her with courtesy and respect. Doing so may result in her referring someone she knows to you. As a romantic who conducts himself with honesty and chivalry, it's okay to try dating a woman and then scaling it back if necessary.

Chapter 8

HOW DO I SHOW HER THAT I LOVE HER?

"I would rather have had one breath of her hair, one kiss from her mouth, one touch from her hand, than eternity without it." – Dana Stevens

Dating should continue until your conversations deepen into the more personal aspects of your lives: your dreams of the future, your fears, your frustrations, and your faith.

<u>Always</u> treat her like a princess: keep up the chivalry, compliments, and romantic gestures. This is especially important once she begins sharing the darker, more painful experiences of her past. We all have them: she needs to know that you will still respect her as she opens her heart to you. Likewise, you need to begin opening your heart to her.

If you feel you're both ready to move into more serious things, then you can keep up the romance but slowly introduce light, playful flirting to the mix.

Flirting is an art form of its own and goes far beyond mere sexual suggestion or innuendo. In fact, it's the art of suggestion... without actually suggesting anything! The objective of flirting is to get <u>her</u> thinking about intimacy while being seemingly innocent.

Flirting could be something as simple as telling her she has a hair out of place as you slowly reach your hand out to put it back in place behind her ear, allowing your hand to brush along her hair to her neck as you look in her eyes and smile.

It could be an innocent comment that, in another context, would be suggestive... play the innocent party and let HER mind do the dirty work!

More than anything, though, you need to let her know that you highly value her companionship, your time with her, and the experiences you share together. If she expresses the same sentiment about you, then you might let her know that you enjoy getting lost in her captivating eyes, and that her lips look so kissable.

Hopefully, you both can get to that deep, intimate kiss.

You also need to <u>slowly</u> build on your relationship until there are few, if any, secrets or off-limits topics remaining. If the subject of sex comes up, be honest with your answers to her questions but again: don't dwell on sex and don't get into too much intimate detail. Tell her you're so glad you both feel comfortable enough to discuss anything and everything with each other, but there are some things you feel should wait... just a little longer. Why?

Despite what popular culture may scream, what you have between your navel and your knees is <u>your sacred ground</u>. The same goes with her. So many people have shared every part of their body with others... but have never opened their heart or shared their soul with another. They're often miserable as a result of that decision because there's nothing left for them to offer The One.

Save it. Encourage her to save it. It will be so much more valuable and worthwhile!

Today's life makes it very easy to hide our fears, failures, and weaknesses. Social media posts and profiles make it easy for us to present only the best in ourselves... and not our entire selves.

When you commit yourself to a deep, intimate relationship with The One, you <u>must</u> expose your weaknesses to her. Your primordial, irrational fears; the pains of your past; your failures and limitations. As you let down your guard and allow her to see your entire humanity, the good and the bad, she will invite you deeper into *her* humanity. The good and the bad.

It's critical that you express the value you place on the trust you share with her. She needs to know that you are her safe refuge: that person with whom she can tell her deepest, darkest secrets without fear that you will judge her or betray her and tell others. Conversely, you need to completely trust her with your deepest, darkest secrets.

If one or both of you don't feel comfortable enough to do that, then you need to slow things down: your relationship is not yet strong enough to get any more serious. Get back to the basics and continue to slowly, but gently and lovingly, explore the reasons why that deep mutual trust isn't yet present between the two of you.

It could be an abusive past with broken trust, or a close friend's or family member's betrayal. A relationship that shattered bitterly. Perhaps even a death or loss of a loved one. Recovering from that can be a slow and painful process... remember, it's not a microwave relationship! If she's still dealing with something that traumatic, explain to her that you will be right there beside her, supporting her as she goes through the grief/coping process or counseling.

You must be able to relate with each other at the deepest, most intimate emotional level if you want a serious, lasting relationship.

Once the two of you feel that you're both ready to truly commit (and that means permanently–for the rest of your lives), then buy her an engagement ring. Arrange the most romantic evening of her life and pop the question. There are plenty of resources on romantic proposals, and meaningful ways you can ask her to marry you.

If she says "yes", then congratulations to you both! Marriage, however, is not something to be taken lightly... nor is it temporary. This is a major, life-disrupting event for both of you. For the rest of your lives! You will most definitely want to schedule pre-marital counseling, with a qualified professional counselor or clergy, who can guide you through the many details involved in this event.

Know going into this that there will be some personal conflict as two very different individuals come together as a married couple. She will need to get her last name legally changed to yours. You'll need to combine your bank accounts and incomes; determine living arrangements and what personal effects stay and what go; assign each other as insurance beneficiaries... it's very complicated! For all the trouble and effort, however, it will all be very, very much worthwhile.

Why?

Consider, for a moment, two highly reactive gases: Hydrogen and Oxygen. They're each very flammable... light a match around either and they will explode in a huge ball of flames. If you combine them, however, with just the right chemistry, they become something that's not only stable, and something that puts out fire, the two gases completely change state into something entirely different.

They become <u>water</u>.

ROMANCE AND CHIVALRY IN MODERN SOCIETY

Hydrogen and Oxygen, two volatile elements that combine into something that neither could ever hope to be individually.

That's why chemistry in a relationship is so vital! A long-lasting relationship isn't based on physical attraction or shared intellectual interests... it's based on something much deeper. Together, the two individuals in a married couple can become something completely different, so much better and more stable, than anything either person could accomplish on their own.

Does that mean that when we get married, we lose our individual identity? No, of course not. That water still has hydrogen and oxygen in it. They're still there, but the bond they share with each other makes each of them better and stronger.

Sure, you could consider the many other women out there... billions of them. Some may be rocket scientists; some are supermodels; some are heiresses to vast fortunes. But they don't have what *your* Lady has. She holds the other part of YOU. The chemistry the two of you have together marginalizes everything else, and everyone else, in comparison.

When you have that sort of chemistry, you need to fight for it and defend it with everything you've got. That means that no one talks badly about your Lady without dealing with YOU—because that's your Queen they're talking about. You will fight her battles and you will slay her dragons... because she's worth it.

Your Lady has a responsibility in this, as well. She'd better not let ANYONE talk badly about you, her man. Not her best friend, not her mother, no one! She saw something in you that compelled her to make a lifetime commitment to you, so now you're both on the hook to grow and nurture your relationship into something that everyone around you will admire.

Prove your skeptics wrong.

So, enjoy the chemistry you and your Lady have–celebrate it! Because sometimes, that's what's going to get you through the rough patches. And you <u>will</u> have them.

Those skeptics, whether they're close to you or to her, may have to be bid farewell if they are merely determined to rob you of your future joy with your Lady. Jealousy can be a vicious thing, especially if they feel that she is getting in the way of your relationship with them (and it rightly should).

That said, make sure you carefully consider their objections to your relationship with her. They may be looking out for you and have valid points. It has long been said that "love is blind" and they may be ensuring that you go into your marriage with "both eyes open", helping protect you from potentially being manipulated and taken advantage of.

Chapter 9

BE THAT COMMITTED GUY

"A true man does not need to romance a different girl every night, a true man romances the same girl for the rest of her life." – Ana Alas

WARNING: there will be disagreements. There will be arguments. There will always be some level of conflict in an intimate, marital relationship because you're bringing two very different individuals into a union of the two. This isn't like a two-piece puzzle and the pieces just fit together perfectly: while that happens, it's incredibly rare. Marriage is more like trying to put a square peg in a round hole. There's friction, there's resistance, and something has to give.

That's why communication and compromise are <u>crucial</u>! You need to let go of some things (and perhaps even some people) from your past... and so does she. This is the objective of good pre-marital counseling: to prepare you both for the conflicts to come.

"Conflict" doesn't mean anger and violence, however. It means talking with each other, understanding each other's point of view and priorities, and working with your new spouse to bring two very unique lives together. Always approach disagreements with love and mutual respect: and never, ever give up and consider divorce as an option because "it's just too difficult". So many new couples do that, and it's sad to see that their first major agreement as a couple is to admit failure over their so-called "irreconcilable differences".

By repeatedly going through the process of conflict resolution in love and respect, however, the bond you share will become stronger, more durable, and your love for each other will deepen. Don't cheat yourselves out of your destined relationship because you chose to quit at the first sign of trouble!

Also: NEVER betray her trust, even if she betrays yours! Once you let each other in, the information you have is never, ever, to be used as a weapon. Even threatening to disclose those "dirty little secrets" during an argument is a great way to instantly destroy everything the two of you have worked to build all this time. Even if you both would never actually tell another soul, the idea that one of you MIGHT is enough to wipe out all the trust the two of you ever shared.

She needs to know that you solemnly promised to be her safe place–and the things she tells you in intimate confidence are things she needs to know you will take to your grave with you, no matter what. You need to be equally confident that all your deepest secrets are safe with her.

Trust isn't only about the information you share with each other: it's also about the physical intimacy you share. No one else has the privilege of going all the way into the person you are like she does: she alone holds the key to your heart, mind, and body. You expect her to be faithful, without anyone else sharing the same level of intimacy with her, right? She expects, and deserves, no less from you.

That means your body is yours, and hers, and no one else's. Her body is hers, and yours, and no one else's.

It's okay to have friends of the opposite sex, as long as they're friends with BOTH of you. If a friendship starts getting uncomfortably friendly for either of you, then it's too friendly. Ease back on that friendship–because there is no friendship more important or valuable than your intimate relationship with the woman you love.

And let's talk about that word–LOVE. Read this very carefully. Then read it over & over until you memorize it, because some guys don't understand the difference between "Love" and "Romance".

"Love" and "Romance" are two completely different things. You can love your woman every day: but romancing your woman every day is so much better. Love is an emotion you *feel*, but that doesn't mean she feels your love for her. Romancing her allows her to do that. You love her and she knows it. Every day.

This is a philosophy you can always trust to be true:

Love is not a noun. It's not something you can have or possess... it's not some hole you can fall into or out of.

Love is a VERB. It's an action you deliberately choose to take, every day, whether you feel like it or not.

No matter what your day holds in store, determine up front, early on, that you are going to love your Lady... no matter what. You may not be happy about that: you may be a bit upset with her. Perhaps she's upset with you... but choose to love your covenant partner through the ups and downs. Love your Lady.

Chapter 10

A LIFETIME OF JOY

"Do I love you? My God, if your love were a grain of sand, mine would be a universe of beaches." – William Goldman

As exciting as the early encounters with her were, as thrilling as your courtship of her was as the two of you grew more familiar and closer, a lasting, long-term marriage should be no less. Never stop courting her. Never stop the pursuit.

It may seem counterintuitive to continue chasing something you've already caught... but that's the mistake made by so many married men when they decide the chase is over and there's no longer a need to romance and surprise their Lady. This can result in a home filled with quiet desperation and self-doubt: with each wondering if they truly made the right decision and married the person meant for them.

Continuing to pursue your Lady requires a complete paradigm shift, and romance is an important part of that shift. Your Lady must be the queen of your life: mind, body, and soul... the center of your universe in this world. Once that shift takes place, you won't stop thinking of ways to pamper her and rock her world. Poems, flowers & cards for no reason, world-class foot massages, little notes by her coffee cup... the possibilities are endless! If nothing else, just let her talk–and genuinely *listen* to her.

Romance isn't about the big, expensive things. It's about the small things, day to day, that cost little to nothing–but make a relationship so worthwhile. They're the things reminding her that, out of the four billion women on Earth, no one else could take her place in your life.

ROMANCE AND CHIVALRY IN MODERN SOCIETY

So many men, who have been married for a long time, treat Valentine's Day like every other day. It's good that you're reading this book because you won't be the sort of husband that wives complain about never being romantic. You will be the sort of husband that your wife's friends will complain their husbands *aren't*.

Valentine's Day should be like every other day: but only because every day should be like Valentine's Day.

That's why it's critical to <u>never</u> stop treating your Queen like royalty. Pamper her, surprise her in little ways (and big), and never give her a reason to doubt her decision to marry you. Woo her then, now, and tomorrow.

Secret Number One to a Long and Successful Marriage

A marriage isn't just a legal arrangement: it's a covenant relationship, established by our Creator, between two people who each possess one-half of the marriage. The husband is better at some things than the wife–and the wife is better at some things than the husband.

Men tend to be logical and visual, operating in the five senses. Women tend to be intuitive and more perceptive to emotions. Men tend to <u>think</u> their way through things; and women tend to <u>feel</u> their way through things.

That is not to say that men don't have feelings or women can't think... that's <u>not</u> the point at all. The core *maternal* instinct, however, is to nurture our young and raise them with love: while the core *paternal* instinct is to protect & provide for our family, teach our young how the world works, and how to solve problems and fix things when they break. That's a broad generalization and, of course, there are exceptions... but when combined in a strong marriage, it gives both a much better perspective of the world around us because we each perceive things the other may not.

We're wired differently, and we're made differently: men and woman are supposed to be different! Again: if two people in a relationship are exactly the same, one of them would be unnecessary, right?

So, a healthy, peaceful marriage is rooted in love and mutual RESPECT.

Too many people believe, often through the examples of their parents and grandparents, that the roles within a married couple is for one to dominate the other, to aggressively lord over their spouse and boss them and their kids around. While we know that there are abusive wives out there, this is a trait primarily seen in the husbands. That makes for a tense home environment that isn't good for anyone, it isn't safe or loving; and it isn't a good example of what a healthy, happy, peaceful marriage is. The role of the husband is to be the spiritual head of the household, and to serve his wife and children as a steward, not as a boss. Fellow man, we can humble ourselves and serve our family in love without being submissive.

Since women are good at relating, you need to know that she is going to tell you all about problems that she does not want you to solve. Most men's first instinct is to listen to the problem, analyze it, develop potential solutions, and implement the best one. Don't do that! She wants to TALK with you about the problem, that's all! If she wants your help solving it, she'll ask you to help solve it. Otherwise, just hold her and say, "wow, Baby, that sounds awful…" and let her talk through it.

We guys, on the other hand, are generally short on words. Most of us are not talky people. We observe the world around us, take it all in, and look for problems we can fix. For example, if you walk into a doctor's waiting room and notice a picture on the wall tilted just a few degrees, will it drive you crazy until you walk over to it and straighten it?

The point is that we men usually don't have a lot to say: when you DO say something, make sure it complies with the letters in the word THINK:

Is it Thoughtful?

Is it Helpful?

Is it Informative?

Is it Nice?

Is it Kind?

THINK. Thoughtful, Helpful, Informative, Nice, Kind. If it's not one of those, then THINK twice before saying it. Chances are, you don't really need to.

While we guys usually don't say a lot, we may DO a lot. We may not tell our Lady that we love her as often as she wants or needs to hear it... but we tend to do things we believe demonstrate that love. Big things, little things. Yes, expressions of our love make up a large component of romance.

However: also remember her need to *hear* you say her name: especially if you use her name in the context of how much you love and adore her, respect her for who she is, and how you couldn't live without her. That's why it's crucial to *communicate* your love and respect, and not just *demonstrate* it. It's equally crucial that you *tell* her how much you love her. Both words and actions are important... and sincerity is everything!

Secret Number Two to a Long and Successful Marriage

It may seem crazy at first, but this is just as important as Secret Number One! There are five magic words to a long and happy marriage, and you need to memorize them:

G. LAMAR WILKIE

<u>SORRY, HONEY, I WAS WRONG</u>

That's it! You're wrong! Even if you *know* you're right, you're wrong—hang up your stubborn pride and just say it! Those five simple words will diffuse so many arguments and fights if you just prevent them at the start and humbly admit fault! It costs nothing!

Your wife will immediately come down off the defensive: it creates a kind of a cease-fire situation in which you can start a dialog to understand each other's point of view. You're both probably looking at the exact same thing, just from two different perspectives. Admitting you're wrong doesn't go on your permanent record, but it does open the door to communication... and communication is everything in a relationship. Because you're relating, and that means you're communicating.

Chapter 11

ROMANTIC TIPS TO GET YOU STARTED

"Never love anyone who treats you like you're ordinary." – Oscar Wilde

A lot of men think that marrying the Princess is the end of the story–if that's you, then you've been watching way too many movies. As we have already discussed, there's a never-ending second part of the story called "Keeping Your Queen Happy". It's not the big, expensive occasions, either... it's the little details, every day, that make a marriage worth being in and staying in. Most of these things cost little to nothing.

Sometimes it doesn't take much for her to know how you feel about her. Leave her a voice message at work; write her a short poem; send her a text message, letting her know you can't stop thinking about her; or even buy an ad in the local paper for her birthday or anniversary. Go out of your way to let her know how you feel. If other people witness it, good for them! Almost everyone appreciates seeing sincere expressions of true love.

EXAMPLE: if I leave home early, my Darling Bride may wake up and find a little note, written on a simple yellow sticky, next to her coffee cup. Or it may be attached to the bathroom mirror. I may slip it into one of her clothing drawers, so I know she'll find it. You don't have to be a poet: just a simple "I love you and can't wait to see you again" will suffice. She may sit down in her recliner and notice an arrangement of fresh flowers and a card on the coffee table... for no reason at all, other than to remind her that I love her.

Yes, I still call her my "Darling Bride" because she is. When many people hear that term, they assume we were recently wed and ask when we got married. They're often surprised to learn that she has been my Darling Bride since December 1990.

Due to the demands of many societies on Earth, women are generally expected to shave parts of their bodies that many men don't... their legs, for example. An incredibly romantic thing for you to do is to shave her legs for her. This is a perfect compliment to your preparing a romantic bath for her: with some bubble bath, bath oil and mineral salts. Perhaps with some candles, soft music and a romantic beverage.

This requires that you gain exceptional skill with your razor; it also requires her to trust you to give her silky smooth legs without nicking or cutting her. In addition to being romantic, it can also be quite erotic for both of you. When she knows she can fully trust you with the razor to shave her legs, she may ask you to shave her underarms or bikini line, as well. If she asks and you feel adequately skilled, do it... and thank her for her trust in you.

Another idea is to write "I LOVE YOU", in big letters, across the bathroom mirror with the corner of a bar of soap before she goes in for her shower. She won't really see it until she gets out of the shower and the whole mirror is fogged up EXCEPT for the letters. Her heart will absolutely melt, and it didn't cost you a thing. You can also sneak in, quickly write it with a dry erase marker and sneak out, while she's in the shower. It's not so much what you do–it's the fact you made the effort to do it that matters most (and please don't make her clean the mirror afterwards).

If you aren't the creative type, don't worry. There are plenty of resources available online with romantic ideas that will have all her friends' husbands quietly raging at you for making them look bad... because she is going to talk about how romantic you are. It's okay to be mushy and lavish affection on your wife: in fact, it's really, really fun! And the rewards for doing so are AWESOME.

(You can always take their husbands aside later and tell them about this book.)

Here are some other ideas:

COFFEE IN BED

If your Lady needs to wake up early, have coffee brewing a few minutes in advance. Take a cup of coffee to her in bed. Lots of extra points if you have a serving tray designed for bed dining, and wake her with a light breakfast of coffee, pastry, sliced fruit, and maybe a small bowl of berries & yogurt. Look online for ideas and ways to arrange the tray for a perfect presentation.

If she doesn't have to wake up early but you must leave while she's still asleep, leave a note by her cup. It doesn't have to be long or poetic: just let her know that you love her and will be thinking about her sweet smile during the day. Send her a text message later and let her know you look forward to looking into her eyes again, holding her in your arms and enjoying the scent of her hair while she rests her head on your chest.

When you get home, do exactly that.

ROMANTIC DINNER FOR TWO AT HOME

It doesn't take a lot of money to be romantic. Sometimes all it takes is a quiet, romantic dinner at home.

If she's having a rough week at work, secretly plan a nice dinner. It can be whatever her favorite dish is, paired with fruit, salad and perhaps a nice wine.

Get home well in advance and prepare for her arrival. Set the table nicely (you can get information on table settings online) and prepare the meal in stages so that everything is freshly made for her.

When she comes home, be clean, freshly shaved and neatly dressed. Have soft, romantic instrumental music playing. Meet her at the door with a kiss and a glass of wine or her favorite beverage. Invite her to get cleaned up and refreshed before joining you for dinner.

When she joins you, dim the lights if possible. If you have candles on the table, light them. Have an arrangement of her favorite flowers on the table. Use your finest dinnerware, cloth napkins, crystal stemware... remember, this is a special occasion, just for her!

Seat your Lady and serve a light first course of fruit and nuts, or perhaps some crackers and cheese. Let her tell you about her day, so she can vent her frustrations and decompress. Tell her that it's okay: you respect and admire the hard work she does, but she's safe with you and you won't let work get to her anymore. Not here, not now, not with you there with her.

Clear the dishes and serve the second course, which might be a small salad with bread. Let her know that you have been thinking about her, and how much you love and adore her. Tell her that you have been planning this dinner as a special occasion at home, for no other reason than you're crazy about her... and that's reason enough.

Clear those dishes and serve the main course. Allow time for both of you to enjoy it. Tell her you hope she savors and enjoys her food the way you savor and enjoy her love and her kisses. Be the romantic!

When the main course is finished, clear the dishes again and follow up with coffee and dessert. It could be a slice of cheesecake, pie, or whichever favorite of hers pairs well with dinner.

Retire to the sofa or bed. Keep the soft instrumental music playing. Slowly disrobe her, kissing her shoulders, arms, and legs, and give her a sensual, loving massage from head to toes, front to back. Massage away any remaining stress and tension and give her a romantic evening she will remember for years. Save the dishes for later: your night may be just beginning! Or she may drift off to a happy, restful sleep. Let her get that much-needed rest.

ROMANTIC NOTES

If you are traveling for a few days (even over a weekend), write a series of short notes on individual slips of paper. Number the notes (1 of 12, 2 of 12, etc.) and hide them in places around your home, her vehicle... maybe even her workplace if you can access it, where she is likely to find them throughout the time you're gone. One could be in her purse, another in the dinnerware drawer in the kitchen, another under the TV remote or her phone. Let it be her little adventure to find all your romantic notes before you return. If she does, she wins the prize! What's the prize? That's a question that only you can answer.

WORLD CLASS FOOT MASSAGE

Many women work all day and are on their feet, walking around, for most of it. By the time they get home they're exhausted: even stay-at-home housewives and mothers are worn out at the end of their day. A skillful footrub can turn her stressful day into a wonderful night.

This involves more than just rubbing her feet. Take the time to learn *reflexology*, which dates back thousands of years and correlates specific areas of her feet and hands to other parts of her body. It follows, then, that the stress on her feet also stresses the rest of her... and vice versa.

It may take you an hour or two to learn the basics of reflexology... and several more hours to master it. You can be confident, however, that your precision and loving care in giving her exactly the relief she needs and deserves, will further strengthen the bond you share.

Start at her knees and massage her calves, soothing away the tension. Let her tell you about her day, venting her frustrations as you massage her. Don't try to analyze her problems and propose solutions: just listen and let her talk it out and decompress. As you feel the tension ease in her calves, move to her ankles and then to her feet. There are plenty of resources available about reflexology, so learning it should not be difficult. Massaging her arms and hands, in the same way, is a perfect compliment to this romantic and intimate technique.

PAPER TISSUE HEARTS

Early in our marriage, we didn't have a lot of money. I secretly bought several packages of red, pink and white gift-wrapping tissue. While on break at work, I would cut out little paper hearts. Lots of them, every day. Once my coworkers understood what I was doing, they helped! We cut out untold <u>hundreds</u> of paper hearts. I took them home in a box and hid them away.

I had told my Darling Bride that I wanted to take her on a coffee date for our first anniversary, after we both finished work. I got home before she arrived, turned off the ceiling fans in our living room and bedroom, climbed a ladder and stacked dozens of paper hearts on top of each fan blade in both rooms. I had a bucket with a bottle of champagne hidden away and poured ice into the bucket to begin chilling it.

She got home, we quickly cleaned up and got dressed, then walked out to the car. I started the car but then told her I'd left my wallet in the bathroom (I actually had, so I wouldn't be lying) and ran back inside while she waited. I quickly moved the chilled champagne bucket & glasses to the bedroom, scattered more paper hearts in a path from bedroom to living room, and from there to the front door. We then left home and had coffee at a nearby coffee shop. We talked over coffee and frugally shared a slice of cake.

When we returned home, she walked in to find hundreds of white, pink and red paper hearts scattered all over the floor in a path leading to the living room. We kicked off our shoes. I walked to the stereo and started our favorite romantic song. We began to slow dance to the music: as we turned, I reached out and flipped the wall switch to turn on the ceiling fan. We danced slowly as hundreds more paper hearts rained down on us. It took her breath away!

After our slow dance, she was almost in tears with the thought of all the effort I'd put into cutting out all those hearts, just for her. We followed the paper heart trail to the bedroom, where champagne and glasses awaited at bedside. After we disrobed and she settled in, I popped the cork and poured champagne for the two of us, and then flipped on the ceiling fan before climbing into bed with her. We toasted each other as hundreds more paper hearts rained down on us. Then I gave her a head-to-toes massage.

She has kept a few of those little paper tissue hearts, all these decades, as a fond memory of my efforts on her behalf.

Chapter 12

CONCLUSION

"The most important things are the hardest to say... because words diminish them." – Stephen King

The true objective in all this is for your Lady to feel like she is the most loved, the most treasured and adored, the most attended-to woman on Earth. Not just on those special occasions like anniversaries, birthdays, or Valentine's Day, but every single day... for the rest of her life.

When you're married with a woman who truly feels that loved, she will have little problem showing that love back to you. She may not be as creative or expressive about it. She may not think of all the romantic things she could do for you. Nevertheless, know that she will come to love and treasure her relationship with you above anything else in the world.

That sort of positive synergy between the two of you will keep you in love for life. You will grow older together and still hold hands as you walk; steal kisses, no matter where you are or who's watching; and be young at heart: spontaneous, daring, and crazy in love with each other every single day. That's worth all the effort you will ever put into it.

I trust you've gained some insight into what romance is; and why it's so important in any intimate relationship. That romance is inside you–it has always been there–and now it's time to bring it to the forefront and make it your primary mindset.

With the new romantic perspective you have, go put it into practice. Every day when you wake up, start thinking about new ways to demonstrate both chivalry to the world at large; and romance to The

One. Consider things you might do and how they may be perceived by the recipient of those things.

Start reading books and websites featuring romantic ideas for men and pick out a few that you think both match your personality and would be well received by your Lady. Schedule them on your calendar, if necessary, and give yourself time to prepare for them. Even if your Lady comes home in a bad mood; or if illness or a family catastrophe shatters the occasion, you can always reschedule things. She and her priorities <u>must</u> come first, all the time and every time.

It's time to go forth and BE THE ROMANTIC you know you are, and never stop.

ROMANCE & CHIVALRY ARE NOT DEAD!

About the Author

G. Lamar Wilkie is a retired U.S. Navy Chief and mushy, romantic husband of his Darling Bride Donna since 1990. Together they have two grown kids, son Christopher and daughter Athena. He wrote a book for each of them when they were young; both books are now published. He enjoys writing; music; is active in church, local civics, and veterans' organizations. He and Donna share a passion for helping others. And for each other.

Cover Art

The cover photo "The Two Candles" was taken by the author February 14, 2022, on the deck of their home. The back cover image "Wine at Sunset" was designed with an AI graphics engine.

G. LAMAR WILKIE

Also by G. Lamar Wilkie

A Man's Guide to Babies

ISBN 978-0-9971141-2-6

A Puppy for Athena

ISBN 978-0-9971141-0-2

Christopher's Tornado

ISBN 978-0-9971141-1-9

Truth or Myth – Deception of the Ages (with Dr. Jimmy Graham, Out of Print)

ISBN 1-882185-14-5